WINDOWS 11 FOR SENIORS

THE ULTIMATE BEGINNER'S GUIDE TO MASTER

YOUR NEW PC. LEARN WINDOWS 11 WITH LARGE TEXT

AND STEP-BY-STEP ILLUSTRATED EXPLANATIONS

D1709395

LIAM DESANTIS

CONTENTS

Introduction to Windows 11

Hi there! It's so nice to meet you. Are you ready to get started learning all of the amazing things Windows can help you do? In today's technological world, it's more important than ever to be able to quickly log on and be able to access a world of knowledge right at your fingertips. I still remember having to dig through the index of the leather-bound set of Encyclopedia Britannica's, pulling the heavy tomes off the shelves just to find the answer to an important question.

I'm not suggesting that there's anything wrong with the approach, it has served the human race just fine for many years. But now, just imagine with a few clicks to have all of the information you could possibly want to see within seconds and a less cardio-inspiring method. Windows 11 has the ability to be able to connect you with countless resources to help you save time, protect your health and finances, and even help you connect with those you love all over the world. The possibilities are truly endless! You can even download a game about birds with anger problems who take on these little green pigs.

In this book, we will see the easiest, less complicated way to get where you want to go, either on your laptop or on the internet. No muss, no fussing around, and the best part of all? We aren't going to give you a bunch of technical jargon that sounds like we are coming from planet Mars.

So, grab a cup of your most favorite coffee and let's settle in for a quick chat between friends. Your personalized support is on the way!

Going Back To Where It Began

The first version of Windows hails from the era of hair bands, Aqua Net, and all things spandex. Or that time period of civilization, 1985. Microsoft founder Bill Gates came up with a brilliant concept, and he made his dreams a reality. He even made using a mouse a popular way before they were standard equipment for any computer set up. Needless to say, the first version of the Windows Operating System looks a little dated now, but everyone has to start somewhere. Now we are presented with a much more modern and streamlined interface, there are countless features and customizations available to make utilizing your computer much more user-friendly and intuitive. Below you will see a representation of Windows 11.

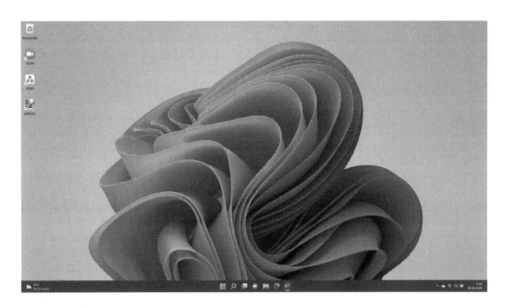

Figure 01

This image will be the basic layout of your device; it may vary depending on if you are using a desktop versus a laptop, or even a tablet. But the basics remain the same across all devices. Once you get the hang of one, you will be able to easily tackle them all with confidence.

If your screen doesn't look like the one above, then you might not be currently running this version of Windows. Not a problem, we'll walk through the easiest way to check this out. However, if you don't have the Windows 11 version currently installed in your PC you can still take a lot of value from reading this book.

Usually, for simplicity's sake, the quickest way to determine this is to click on the Start menu. To access the Start menu you just have to click on the icon with the Windows logo (it looks like four little squares). Click then on the This PC tab, which will give you all of the important specs of your device. For example, you should be able to find the requirements to see if they match the components necessary for installing Windows 11 if you are not already currently running the program. The basic requirements can be found on Microsoft website. Alternatively, you should also be able to read the requirements on the back of the Windows 11 box or on the information leaflet that came with it.

But that's just a bunch of tech mumbo jumbo, right? It still doesn't answer our question too much. So the quick way to determine if your computer is compatible and able to install the new Windows is to download an app called PC Health Check, and once that is installed on your device, it will make finding all of the information you need regarding the components of your computer easy as pie. We will go over this more in the chapter that discusses how to download apps to your device and what ones are safe and useful.

For the rest of the step-by-step guide, we are just going to assume that you already have this version of Windows installed and that we are ready to get started. It's time to take that first step down the technological interstate, there are some important things to stop and see along the way, I won't tell you it's as majestic as Route 66, but there's a lot to learn along the way.

CHAPTER 1

Navigating & Basic Features

Compared to a lot of the older Windows programs, there have been a lot of changes in order to make devices running Windows more approachable and user friendly.

Figure 02

The new Start screen and the widgets at a glance section that will appear off to your left are going to be one of the more recent updates to the program and really help keep things organized. You can see what the weather is, your to-do list features photos, and even stay caught up on the news. These separate components are called widgets, and you are able to customize your device to only display what you want to see. You just have to look through the available options and see what works for you. If you click on the icon shown in the image above as the two rectangles, you can customize your widgets and how they appear.

Along the bottom, you see the icons; these are programs that have either come preinstalled on your device or, if you download an app, they will often appear on this bottom bar. To use one of the programs, all you have to do is click on it, and the program will start up.

One quick example is, you see the magnifying glass down there? On that one, if you are looking for a specific file...let's say you have a recipe that you stored on the computer or someone saved on the device for you. You click on that magnifying glass, and a search box will appear. Usually, just by inputting keywords like, "Lemon Ice Box Pie" for example, it will bring up anything saved on your computer that contains those words. You can trim down your search by making sure you click on the file that must contain this specific phrasing. But a general search is how I generally go about locating those files that have seemed to go missing. If you are very new to Windows you might wonder what a file is. A file is just a virtual holder of records. In the example above, a file can be a document with your favorite recipe but a file can also be a song, a video, a photo etc.

Other programs that usually come preinstalled on your device are a calculator, an assortment of casual games, like solitaire for example, and a program to either sign in to your already existing email accounts, or to create a new account to help you stay in contact with those around you.

One of the great things of the advancements technology has made is the amount you are able to customize your computer to fit your daily life.

Also shown on the graphic starting this chapter is an example of the box that appears on the screen when you use the Start menu function to search. You just type what you are looking for in the box up above, and it will show you all of our options. Including the helpful Get Started icon. This is a great tutorial on how to get started working with this software and has the ability to show you what is possible. I couldn't possibly talk about everything you might see when you are just starting out. But this is the easiest approach to learning about what specific things/apps and preinstalled programs can do.

As you see from the graphic on the previous page, there's a lot of potential, but let's revisit the customization aspect. Up there, do you see the little gear icon that is your settings, and where you will head if you want to change where the Start menu is if you need to increase the size of the text to make it easier to see, or even turn on the speech to text, or other accessibility settings. You can customize the appearance, for example, if you do not like the picture on your desktop (what picture is showing on the screen that has the icons placed on it). You can change it to whatever you would like, either a wallpaper option that comes standard with the program or your favorite family portrait. The sky's truly the limit.

Working off of the same image here, another thing you will probably want to consider as a first step is creating your Microsoft account, this is an easy process, and they will give you step-by-step prompts to help get you all set up. Some will have you do this when you buy a new computer when you first set it up, but if you happen to purchase a used or refurbished machine, you might have to go in and set one up that way. Either process is relatively simple, creating your account will become necessary later on when we are talking about downloading specific apps or saving any spreadsheets, pictures, or scanned in financial documents to the cloud storage.

But from the start point, when you first turn the computer on for the first time, it will resemble every other device running this program, it's only when you begin to customize your settings that the device really becomes tailored to your needs.

So, you just turned your computer on, you've got your Microsoft Account set up, you've got a pretty solid grasp on the functions of the desktop, and how to navigate to your settings in order to change things around if you so wish. Let's take a look at another powerful tool that is part of the desktop. If you look to the right-hand corner of the screen down at the bottom you will see the time and date function. Next to that there is the quick settings area, which gives you basically the pulse of your computer.

Figure 03

It will show you how much battery is remaining if you are a laptop or tablet, volume levels are right next to it, your Wi-Fi settings are next, along with microphone settings and Bluetooth, in case you want to connect to your phone or another device in close proximity. Anything you might need to check if something isn't functioning right can be found here and is an essential troubleshooting tool.

This guide has a chapter designed to help you connect your devices as well as one on the use of the Internet. However, just to give you the basics now the Wi-Fi is the technology used to connect your computer to the Internet while the Bluetooth technology allows you to connect devices such as your computer and an external keyboard.

There are some basic actions that you will want to be aware of just starting out, the ability to copy and paste is essential, and for that, there are a few specific usages. If you desire to copy and paste some information from a website, you would just select the text and then right-click, and it will bring up some actions. Copy would be what you want here. Then when you get your text or image highlighted, if you have an email, note, or Word document open, you just have to right-click once you get over there and it will give you the list of options again, this time you would click paste. And there you go!

You just successfully copied and pasted your first text or image. This action is one of those that are irreplaceable; you never really realize how much you use it until you stop and think about it, then it becomes pretty clear! I think I am an avid copy and paster, personally.

Another cool trick to learn is that when you are trying to save an image, you can do it the way I just described, or you can also click and drag the image from its original source, let's say a webpage, just click on the image, then move the arrow over to an unoccupied space on your desktop, and it will copy the image over there as well. I like to use this option if I have some email image attachments; I hate to wait for them to download, and then have to find them in the download folder. So I use this action pretty extensively as well.

Finally, the last action in this chapter we are going to discuss is how to locate your files; this works a little differently than just the search techniques as it opens the This PC tab, and in this one, you can save, rename, move and find all your files of a certain type. So either pictures, documents, music etc. It makes for a one-stop shop for finding what you need when you needed.

From the Start menu, you will right-click and then just click where it says This PC. It should bring up a box that looks like this.

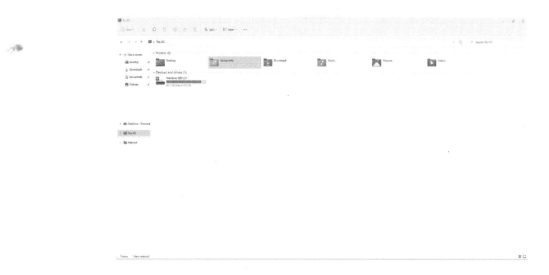

Figure 04

From here, just click on either the file type you are looking for, where you are looking for something, from the column on the left and then because the software is so helpful, it also gives you recent files just to help you return to whatever you were last working on. Now, if you want to create a new folder to save your recipes, for example, you will see on the graphic on the previous page, just click on documents. Then once that loads up at the top, there is a new drop-down menu of actions. You can see on the figure below that up at the top, you will see where it says folder, and just click there.

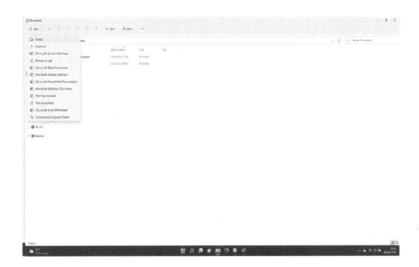

Figure 05

After you have done that, you will see where the new folder pops up, you can rename this by just right clicking, and when the menu of actions pops up, there will be a rename action. This allows you to be able to rename the folder to fit whatever it contains. Having folders it's very useful to keep all your files organized. From now on, you will just have to drag your files in the correct folder you previously created to have a well-organized desktop.

Now that we have made it to the end of the chapter let's take a look back at what we've learned, we embraced the fact that there have been countless iterations of Windows. For the last 37 years, this system has been a part of the human experience. We've scratched the surface on everyday actions you will want to take, like customizing your settings, watching the getting started tutorial and ensuring your Microsoft account is set up and ready to go. We even touched on the different commonly used programs that are on the bottom of your screen.

Look how much we learned in just a few pages. And we've still got more to come! Remember, at any time you can flip back and review some of the steps on how to find the things you are looking for, or how to complete a certain action, or just take a peek at the example graphics to kind of get a feel for how things work. But for now, it's time to head off into the next chapter!

CHAPTER 2

Installing Software

In chapter 2, we will explore how you get those must-have programs onto your computer if it is something it doesn't already come with straight out of the box. This used to be a more complicated procedure, with floppy disks or then the CD-ROM, but now downloading the necessary software is as simple as going to the website and hitting download within a couple of clicks; your device does most of the heavy lifting for you. As an example, I'm going to guide you through a few different examples. We are going to discover how to download a different web browser than the one commonly installed on most laptop/desktop computers. And then after that, we will talk about how to download and install Zoom, a video conferencing/video chat software that has really gained in popularity since the pandemic started with people working remotely and checking in with their boss or co-workers or having family gatherings and just checking in with those you love in a more personal way than just over the phone. After that, we are going to close with why having anti-virus/internet security programs are so important.

Web Browser

Just before starting with the tutorial I want to tell you what a Web Browser is. A Web Browser is simply an application used to navigate the Internet and to then present the information to you in an easy visual way. Web browsers are, for example, Google Chrome, Edge, Safari and Mozilla Firefox.

For the purposes of this specific example, we will be discussing downloading Google Chrome. Our first step is that you will want to locate the Edge icon. This will be on the bottom of your screen. Please, reference the graphic below for what the icon looks like it's the blue and green swirl on the taskbar, second from the end.

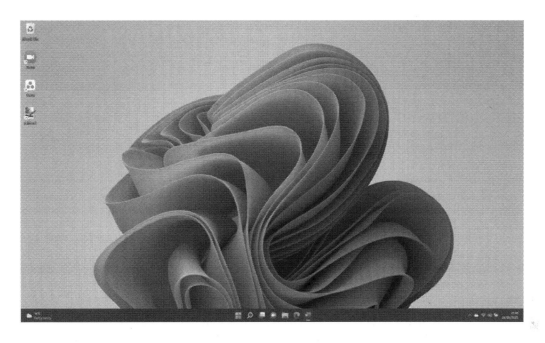

Figure 06

Easy right? So once you have located that icon, go ahead and open it up.

Once it pulls up the browser window, just type the following text string (also called link): https://www.google.com/chrome/

Or you can do a fast Google search for it within the Edge window, and it will bring it up as well. In other words, you can just type "Google Chrome installing" on the Search Bar that will appear once Edge is open.

Once the page loads, there will be a download Chrome button, it's pretty big, you can't really miss it. When you click on that area, another box will pop up. It will say downloads at the top, and it will then ask you what you would like to do with the downloaded file. All you need to do is now to select where it says Save As and click on that box.

It will bring up a file save box, and all you have to do is hit save down at the bottom. And the file will start downloading,

After it finishes downloading, a box will appear, and it will give you an Open File option, click on that button, and the installation process will begin.

It may ask you to input your password or ask if you trust the file, depending on how your settings are configured, in that case, just give approval, and you will be good to go.

Once the installation process is finished up, it should open automatically. If it does not, check for a new icon and then just click on it to open the browser. It will function just like your typical browser, personally, I use Chrome most often, but some people like Edge, which already comes installed on your device, and some people prefer Firefox, it just depends on your preferences, each of them has their perks.

That's all there is to it! This is the basic premise for downloading any software program you might require. Apps are a little different in their process, and that's why we will go over that in a separate chapter. Since we crossed that off our to-do list, for now, let's move on to Zoom.

Zoom Installation

So here, I think it is important to note there are two ways you can download Zoom onto your computer. You can either decide to go directly to the website, and follow much the same process we laid out when discussing how to install Google Chrome, or there is also an app for Zoom that you can download through the Microsoft Store. Whichever option you feel more confident and comfortable with as far as downloading is the path I would take. I have used the web download version as well as the app version, and both work about the same. Just a slight difference or two, which you wouldn't really take note of unless you use it day in and day out. For this chapter, we are just going to talk about downloading the web version since that is within the scope of this chapter.

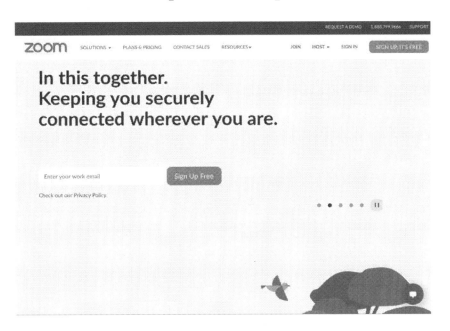

Figure 07

Once again, we are going to navigate to the Edge icon at the bottom of the screen and then click on that to open the program. Next, you will type or paste in this link: https://zoom.us/

If you live in a country other than the US, there would be country-specific links, so you would have to search for the one that suits your location.

But once the page has loaded, you will see the page above. Next, click on resources

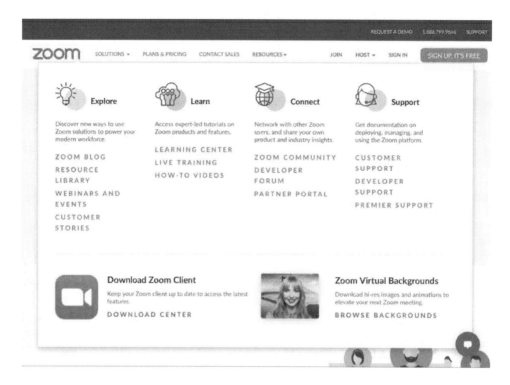

Figure 08

Where it says download Zoom Client click on that one, and basically just follow the prompts as we did with Google Chrome. Hitting Save As, then Save on the following box and wait for the file to finish downloading before opening it and beginning the installation process.

The same rules apply; your device may ask you if you want to install the file, and if that's what you want to do, then approve the installation. Once it finishes up, as with most files, it will open on its own. If it does not, there will be a specific icon for Zoom, and it's actually on a couple of the example images. So if you get stuck on what the icon might look like, just flip back, and you should be able to spot it.

Once you have the program open, it will ask you to set up an account with either a social media account or by email. We will see more about emails in another chapter. When you are getting ready to join your first chat, there will be some additional tweaks necessary to make sure your camera and microphone are functioning correctly. The software does a brilliant job of walking you through the process, and even those not in the slightest tech-savvy are able to make it through the setup with flying colors.

Now you have two software programs under your belt that you are able to download, install and configure. The great thing about technology, and Windows does a great job of this, is helping the person using the device to break down the action in multiple parts so it doesn't seem as intimidating as one might initially think. Nobody has to go making a mountain out of a molehill, you have the ability to manage anything that is thrown at you and just making time to learn how to utilize technology and all of the great things it can do are definitely worth it.

One of the next programs we are going to talk about is adding an internet security or antivirus program to your computer just to keep your sensitive information such as bank account information, social media accounts, passwords, health records...etc as protected as possible.

I'm quite sure by now we have all heard countless stories about this big company being hacked, and the data was breached and floating around out there in cyberspace. Most of these instances are prevented, but there are groups of people who are constantly trying to find a way in. This is why I always recommend to my friends and family to have some kind of protection software on your device. One of the advances Microsoft has made is including Windows Defender. This is a preinstalled anti-virus software, so don't panic and think you were unprotected all this time; there was some level of protection prior to you adding another layer of security to your computer.

Anti-Virus Software

There are many different options when you are comparing anti-virus/internet security programs to protect your identity and information. Norton is used by many people; it's usually the first one you hear about because it seems like as long as there has been the Windows program, there has been Norton right there to back them up. Now, there's nothing wrong with Norton, their anti-virus is top-notch, and with the brand recognition and reputation, you really can't go wrong.

The only con I really see in the anti-virus race is the fact that Norton is rather expensive when compared to some of the other options.

Judging from the articles and reviews I have read it seems the best, all-around anti-virus for Windows 11 users would be a company called Bitdefender. This company has topped a lot of lists in the sector, and it seems to be a good product, it's easy to understand and get set up, and once it's keeping an eye on your computer, you don't have to worry much about any pesky cyber threats.

So, head back to the Edge icon, and once you get the browser window pulled up, then we are going to paste in the following link: https://www.bitdefender.com

Once you reach this page, completing the sign-up is pretty straightforward, simply select the product, or plan you are looking to purchase, and it will guide you through the download process. Once you begin the installation process, it follows the same procedure, and once you have the program open, you are ready to complete the first scan of your system with the new software.

Most programs that include an anti-virus, as well as an Internet security aspect, are multi-purpose. You can initiate a virus scan of the system at any time, but with internet security, it is always on the lookout for anything that might be trying to gain access to your device. Now whether that is someone on the other end of their computer screen trying to access your information, or it is some program that has spyware embedded in the program. Staying on top of the updates for your program is also essential as new threats are being conjured up all the time.

When you are signing up to your favorite anti-virus or another software you are usually asked to insert an Email address and a password (also called log-in credentials or log-in information). This is the normal process when you are registering in a website to access a program like an anti-virus. This process is safe and it will become easier with time. If you don't have an email address already, hold on because we will see how to set up one in another chapter.

Final Thoughts

Now we have detailed how to get through the process of installing software that didn't come pre-installed on your device, it seems pretty straightforward, right? Some software will require you to make an account with them to utilize the program, like Zoom, for example, or for the anti-virus, you must purchase the software and then set up your account. Keeping track of subscriptions or annual plans and all of the log-in information can get to be a hefty task. This is why I still keep an address book or monthly planner in my desk drawer, so when I get a new program that requires either a monthly or yearly subscription plan, I know when the next payment is going to be due. I also write down my log-in information and any other pertinent information just in case someone else needs to handle my affairs; everything is organized and easy for someone to step in and handle.

CHAPTER 3

Let's Go Web Surfing USA

I really couldn't pass up the possibility to pass on a little Beach Boys humor there, but this chapter is going to be dedicated to hitting the World Wide Web and being able to find what you want, weeding out what you do not, and staying safe from those scam websites or scam messages that are targeted at seniors to capitalize on the fact that a lot of the population thinks that just because you've reached a certain age, there is no possible way you could be tech-savvy enough to spot a scam from a mile away.

So let's start with the basics, opening up your web browser, click on the icon of either Edge or Google Chrome or whichever browser you have liked. You will see they all share some basic characteristics. The first page you come to is referred to as the home page. For Chrome, this would be Google, many different browsers will allow you to customize which home page you prefer. For example, I use Google Chrome, and a friend of mine uses Bing because they like the picture of the day. Both are Web Browsers, and both usually have a rundown of trending searches, news stories...etc.

For most of browsers, there is what is called an address bar up at the top, although in recent years this started to be called the search bar as you can perform any search you would like straight from there versus going to Google, or Yahoo itself. Then type in your search, and wait on the results.

One thing you will commonly see is a padlock in this bar when you have a link displayed. This means the site is secure; it will usually possess its own security services, you'll see this a lot with online checkouts. This is also something crucial to keep an eye on when you are trying to determine if a site is a scam or not. If you think that it should be locked down, but it isn't... that's a red flag.

Now, one of the unique capabilities of the newer browsers is that they allow you to open "tabs" each one allows you to look at a different website, or for example, on my browser right now, I currently have a grocery order I'm placing on one tab, and on another, I have my inbox open, and then on a third, I have a blog article I was reading. All varied content and sites, but all things I'm multitasking with right now.

One thing it is important to remember in regards to opening tabs, remember you can close your tabs. Most people think the browser does it for them, some do while others, however, do not. So it's important to close out of the tab by hitting the X on the side of the open tab if you want to close it. Having too many tabs open at one time can slow down the performance of your computer, so if you have things running a little slow, that would be the first thing I would consider checking.

History in the Making

The next thing we are going to tackle in regards to using the web browser, and for this walkthrough, we are using Google Chrome. However, do you ever land on a website and close out of the tab, only to wish you could revisit the page? But the specific address isn't ringing any bells. I call this approach is like throwing away the cooking directions only to 5 minutes later grab them out of the trash to confirm the amount of water. So, luckily if something like that happens, you can go back and look at your browsing history and find exactly where you were and return to the page. How do you do that on Chrome? Let's break this down into sections.

See your history

1. If you are sitting at your computer, click on the icon and open Chrome.
2. At the top right, click **More**. It will have a symbol with three vertical dots.

3. Click **History**, and then again **History**.

It will pop up with what sites you have visited and when Chrome has usually them broken down into dates. For the current day though, it drills down even further and has them separated by sites you visited in the morning, sites in the afternoon...etc.

There may come the point in time where you want to wipe your browser history. This is absolutely necessary because things get so clogged up that it makes your browser run slow, or for example, I always clear my browser history after I'm finished Christmas shopping so people can't go back and see either what I ordered or what I was looking at.

To clear your history

1. If you are sitting at your desktop, click on the icon and open Chrome.
2. At the top right, click **More** and the three vertical dots.
3. Click **History**.
4. If you look to the left, click **Clear browsing data**. A new window will appear.
5. From the menu, you will need to select how much of your history you want to get rid of. If you are going to wipe everything, select **All Time**.
6. Then, you just need to select the checkboxes for the specific information you want to clear. This will include "browsing history."
7. Click where it mentions **Clear Data** to finish the process.

Delete an item from your history

If you are just looking to delete certain things, you can pinpoint what you want to delete from your history. In order to search for something filtered, you will want to utilize the Search bar. This works great for the Christmas present example I listed above,

1. Open Chrome.
2. At the top-right, click on the icon with three dots.
3. Then click where it says **History**.
4. Mark the box next to each item you want to remove from the History.
5. Click up where it says **Delete** at the top right.
6. Finish up by clicking where it says **Remove**.

Now, if you don't want to jump through nine hoops to avoid the beans being spiked about someone uncovering their present, you could use a private browsing tab. But using that option, it doesn't show up in your regular history; it doesn't keep any log-in information saved, basically, it is a clean slate each and every time. If you want to use Chrome private mode you just have to right-click on the Google Chrome icon and click "New Incognito Window". Please, be aware that navigating in private mode doesn't make your computer, or better your IP address if we want to be techy, invisible to external websites. It's just an internal way to not save your previous searches.

For our next important action, it is imperative to know about, placing a bookmark on a webpage. Like its physical counterpart, that's pretty much what placing a bookmark means on a web page. It reminds you where you were; it comes in handy when it is a site that you often frequent. On Google Chrome you can add a bookmark, or add it to your favorites by clicking the star that is toward the top of the page. Alternatively, if you click where the circle that has your initial on it, or profile picture if you uploaded one, most of the time they give you a big sheet of actions you might want to take. It would have a space for it there as well. I know Google gives you a couple of different ways to add a bookmark, but many browsers don't go quite that above and beyond.

How to Recognize an Unsafe Website

There are a few different things you will want to train yourself to keep an eye out for during your web browsing, It's pretty easy to end up on the wrong site, either just a letter or two, either way, this can take you somewhere you definitely didn't mean to be, and hackers and thieves count on this fact as their bread and butter. Taking some extra seconds to evaluate a site before handing over any personal information or making a purchase is essential in today's day and age. So what things are essential to look for? Check out these tips and tricks.

First and foremost, check for the SSL certificate, and make sure your link contains HTTPS and not just an HTTP. We talked about this before, but that extra means that the site is secure by them using an SSL. We won't go into defining all the technical terms, but basically it just boils down to the fact that the site is secured by more than just whatever cybersecurity program you currently have installed.

The next step is to check the link in your address bar, is everything spelled as it should be? Are there other weird typos that are throwing you off? Chances are there might be something funky going on. Luckily there are a couple of ways to check the site out. Some of your anti-virus programs may allow you to check individual sites, but if they do not, you can use Google Safe Browsing, which is part of Chrome already, or if you are using Microsoft Edge, I would recommend using Virus Total it gives you the capability to upload files or simple links to check and make sure that they are on the up and up. It's a great tool, and one I highly recommend for the ease of use, and it always does a great job and checking things thoroughly. Keeping your information safe while browsing, it is essential to pay mind to. I can't think of how many stories I've heard, even within my own family of people who have fallen prey to internet scams. They can look really legitimate, so always do your due diligence and check things out, follow your gut is the best advice I can give here.

Another one to be on the lookout for are the security seals, we've all seen them, usually, there are at least 1-2 on almost every website where you can make a purchase, but how can you tell if they are legitimate or not? It's all too easy for someone just craft a picture into the web design to make it look like it is a legitimate seal. Really on this one, the most common way to check is to click on the seal itself. If it sends you to the company's website that issued it, then it's on the up and up. If it doesn't and sends you somewhere else, or doesn't pop up with anything that is a blaring alarm bell.

The final aspect of evaluating a website is if there are quite a few pop-up ads, flashing banners, and more bells and whistles than the penny slots in Reno. I would make sure no other red flags are popping up, we do live in an age of affiliate programs, which essentially if you own a blog website, for example, companies will pay you to advertise on your website for them. They will then pay you a commission for every sale that is made through your link. So many people will sell this space to a lot of different companies, and then the problem becomes, are they all legitimate? It also makes the page so cluttered and unable to function correctly that the site becomes useless. So, not saying this is an automatic run for the hills if you see this happening unless it's on a site where you have to enter your card or banking information or any other sensitive information. Then you will probably need to find a different option.

Commonly Used Websites

I wanted to add a little cheat sheet of resources that might give you an excellent place to start on sites many people utilize and that are safe sites. These are all US links, so if you live in another country, most of them have custom-tailored sites for the region you live in, so it may just take a quick search to find the site designated for your area.

<u>Amazon</u>: you can get almost anything you need from Amazon, groceries, home goods, pet food, and even your monthly prescriptions. Signing up for an Amazon account is as simple as putting in your email address and creating a password. We will see more on this later if you haven't set up an email address yet.

<u>eBay</u>: I love eBay for finding replacements to some of my china sets or finding that hard-to-find item. Many things are used over here, but usually still in great condition, so if it's something Amazon doesn't carry, eBay will probably have it.

<u>Instacart</u>: This is a delivery service that a lot of grocery stores and places like Walgreens, Wal-Mart...etc use, you just find what you need and pick a delivery time and they will bring your order right in front of your door. They do offer contactless delivery, which I thought was a huge plus.

<u>CNN</u>: Usually, I spend the first hour of my day drinking coffee and getting caught up on the news. I like CNN's global coverage, but there are a lot of news sites out there, like Fox News, and whatever local TV news station you have around. If you really enjoy your local news, I recommend following their pages because I have found many interesting stories that never make it onto the live broadcast. There's always a lot more they post online, and a quick Google search will take you straight to their page.

Final Thoughts

Overall, the internet is a fantastic tool. You should just be aware of some of the pitfalls that you might stumble into. Hopefully, with the information we just went over you will be able to navigate the turbulent waters of surfing the web, and get what you need out of it and escape unscathed. Just remember if something seems funny, take a good look at the content and check it out, or even ask a friend or family member before inputting any information. This way you and your information will be as safe as possible.

CHAPTER 4

You Need an App for That?

There is a long-running joke now that people say, there's gotta be an app for that, or can you believe there is an app for that? The landscape of this industry has skyrocketed. Today, anyone who has a basic knowledge of coding, can create a simple software and upload it on resources like the Microsoft Store. Some apps are free, some require you to pay a small fee before you download the program, and even still, some will charge you to download the app, and then you need to pay a monthly subscription fee as well. Don't get discouraged though, I know it sounds like a trip through the Microsoft App Store will become as spendy as taking a journey through Macy's, but there are a lot of great apps out there that won't break the bank. First, we will discuss how you get to the Microsoft Store, then the process of downloading an app. After that, I'll give some app ideas you might want to try.

Finding the Microsoft Store

As you have seen on some of the other graphics, there is a direct icon to the Microsoft Store. Sometimes it is already on your taskbar (the area at the bottom of your screen with the icons), or you can find it through the Start menu. All you have to do to open the program is tap on the icon to open the program. When the page ended to load up, you should see a screen like the one shown in Figure 10:

Figure 09

Here you have a world of possibilities...everything from apps like Zoom like we discussed before, to Netflix, and other streaming services, to finding classic card and board game apps to play in your spare time. If you can think it up, there is more than likely an app for that. So to start your search, reference the graphic on the previous page. At the top, where you can read search for apps, games, and movies, is where you will put what you are looking for. When whichever app you are looking for pops up, then there will be a button that says Get if it's a free app. If the app costs to download, it will tell you the price instead. All you are supposed to do now is to click the button, and the installation process will begin.

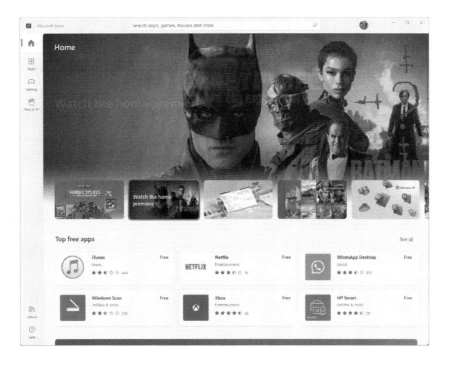

Figure 10

It may ask you once you hit Get, for example, to sign in with your Microsoft Account information, which you should already while setting up your computer. Just use your log-in credentials, and you should be just fine with starting the installation process.

The last couple of important things to note are making sure your apps stay updated, and where can you find the apps you have downloaded?

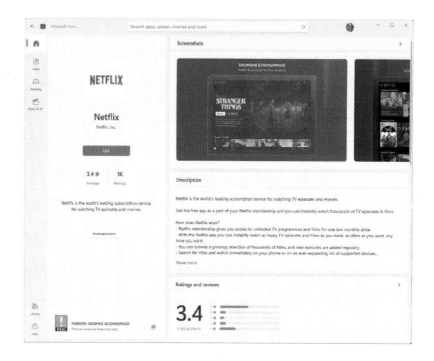

Figure 11

Looking at the graphic above, down in the left corner where there is the icon that looks like a stack of books, that is your library. If you click on that icon, you will see all of the items that have been downloaded to your account. Click on the appropriate tab to find what you might be looking for. For the purposes of the rest of our example, if you click on Apps, it will show you all of the apps that you have. Some if not all, are installed already on your device, but if you end up accidentally deleting an app, or if you get a new device, it's easy to just go to your library and then reinstall the apps you love.

Now, once you get to where the apps tab is, there is a blue button on the right where it says Get Updates. This is important to keep tabs on, it is important to make sure your apps stay updated, as some of them need certain things fixed or add new features. You can choose to get updates automatically, or you can choose to update them manually. If you are currently on a limited data plan with your Internet provider, I would keep auto-updates turned off as they can eat up a lot of your plan data. But if you are with an unlimited data plan, you don't have to worry about it.

But just click on the Get Updates, and any app with a new version available will be automatically updated. You will have the optimum experience the app can offer.

That'll be all there is to it! Open the Microsoft Store, search for what you want, and click Get or Buy depending on which app you are looking to download, and you are ready to use the resource. Enjoy that Netflix binge-watch and kiss productivity goodbye!

Apps to Consider

With the world of apps out there, I just wanted to stop and take a few minutes to give you some categories of apps and within those categories to share some of my favorites.

<u>Entertainment</u>: These are my go-to streaming apps. I especially like Frndly TV and Pluto TV for those older shows you can't find in syndication anymore, like Gunsmoke, Maverick, Home Improvement, Alf..etc. And who doesn't love a good Hallmark movie? Be careful with that one; you might fall down the adorable factor rabbit hole and end up binge-watching the Christmas movies all day. Believe me, I've done it. Again, these are listed on the US site, and I wish I could tell you they are available in all countries or give you more targeted recommendations for those who live across the pond, but on that, I'm just not sure.

- Netflix
- Hallmark Movies Now
- Hulu
- Disney +
- Prime Video
- Frndly TV
- Pluto TV

Delivery Services: a lot of these apps have a regular web version as well, but I always like to mention there are apps for these so if they are services you use quite a bit. It's worth it to have the app instead of just the browser, as sometimes your delivery driver has to send you messages, or tracking your order. It helps to have the app close at hand. Some of these are for big box stores, and some are for if you are looking to order from a local restaurant and you just want it brought to your home. Tractor Supply Co, if you have one local, has an excellent delivery service, and they can bring you pet food, plants, mulch...etc. All those things I hate having to haul around, I will gladly pay a delivery fee just to save some time and wear and tear on my back. One thing to note is that not all areas are serviced by these delivery apps. You will just have to see who offers delivery in your specific area.

- Instacart
- Wal-Mart
- Tractor Supply Co
- DoorDash
- Uber Eats
- Lowe's

Tools: your computer already comes with some basic tools built-in, but going a step further, if there is something you might need, these are the top recommendations.

- Adobe Acrobat
- Microsoft To-Do Lists, Tasks
- Office
- Second Screen
- Screen Magnifier
- Zoom

- Windows Notepad

- Microsoft Journal

<u>Photo Apps</u>: we all have tons of pictures of those special moments in life. These apps will help you organize all of your photos in one place, allow you to order prints of your digital copies, and even scan in and store the physical ones so you have an extra copy in the case of something unforeseen should happen to the original.

- Adobe Photoshop

- Shutterfly

- Picsart Photo Editor

- Affinity Photo

- Photo Scan OCR

- Instagram

<u>Games</u>: I don't know about you, but sometimes I just want to sit down at my computer and decompress. Usually, playing one of my favorite games really helps me unwind after a long day. Here are some of my favorite gaming apps guaranteed to help you decompress!

• Angry Birds

- FarmVille

- Solitaire

- Bingo Blitz

- Slotomania

- Candy Crush Saga

- Wordle

- Brain Test—Tricky Puzzle Game

Final Thoughts

As you can read, this is just a tiny portion of the apps out there that are vying for your attention. You will discover that you can find an app for almost everything from grocery delivery, to having someone come and walk your dog if you aren't able to get out and about to take them out, to reading your favorite book through your local library. The possibilities are truly endless, all you have to do is click on that search bar, and away you go! One thing to remember is that you do only have a certain amount of space on your device, so having 100 apps probably isn't feasible. However, trying them out and then deleting them off your device is as simple as dragging the icon to the recycle bin (it looks like a wastepaper bin with the recycle symbol on it). You can clear them off if you don't think they fit your needs, or you just don't like them. With games, I have a bad habit of doing this! I play one for a month or two, then I get bored with it and move on to another one. The great thing is I can always go back to my library and reinstall the app if I want to revisit it.

CHAPTER 5

Stay Connected with Emails

Today it seems like the whole world revolves around emails. We are waiting for one to drop in our inbox. We are weeding through the advertising emails we get from making an online purchase or places we've signed up to get discounts. We are sending out a multitude of emails a day to our boss, co-workers, or clients if you are lucky enough to manage your own business. It seems like the cycle never ends! It does tend to make one miss the days of writing a letter to someone you wish to talk to and mail it out. But life changes, and society with it. So now, emails are the quickest and most simplistic way to stay in contact with someone.

If you haven't done it already, this chapter is going to walk through setting up your email and utilizing it through the Windows 11 Mail App. This is one of the preinstalled programs already on your device, so we shouldn't have to go through getting it all downloaded.

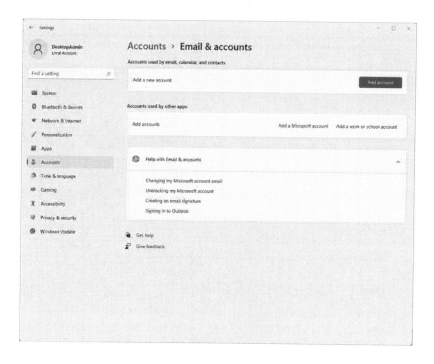

Figure 12

Step 1: usually, when you set up your Microsoft Account, they give you an Outlook or Hotmail email address. It will probably resemble one of these: mrjones@hotmail.com or <u>mrjones@outlook.com</u>. This would be an email address you could use, if you already have an email address through somewhere like Gmail, or Yahoo, or another email provider you can set up the Mail App to use that email address.

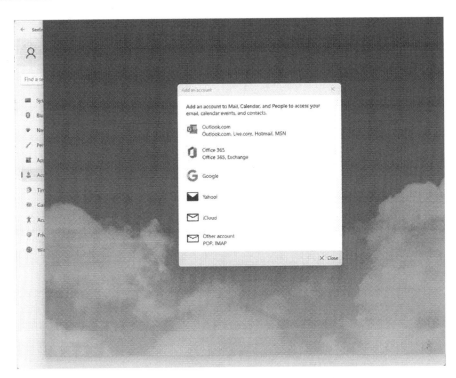

Figure 13

If you think that none of these options work for you, then we will need to create you a new account from scratch, which isn't too hard. You just go to the website of the email provider you wish to use. We will use Gmail for this example. Search Gmail in your search bar on the web browser and it will take you right to the sign-up page, it will mention something about creating an account, and with just a couple of clicks and selecting an easily accessible address, (usually I use names of my pets, or my first and last name so I can always remember what it is) you have set up your email account and you are ready to begin emailing and sending pictures and videos out.

Now, back to setting up the account to use on your computer with the Mail app.

1. Select **Start**, click on the settings icon and then where it says accounts used by Email, Calendar and Contacts.

2. Select **Add account** to get started.

3. Select the brand of the account you want to add. (This is usually shown as what comes after the @ symbol in your email address, so @gmail, or @hotmail).

4. Enter the information on the prompts and click on **Sign in**. For most accounts, the only information you need is the email address, your password, and if you named it something different, the account's name.

5. Select **Done**. Your email account will start copying over as soon as your account is set up. **NOTE: sometimes, the sync process takes a few minutes to finish up, so if it doesn't immediately pop up in your inbox, it may still be working on it.**

These steps are shown graphically on Figures 12, 13, 14 and 15

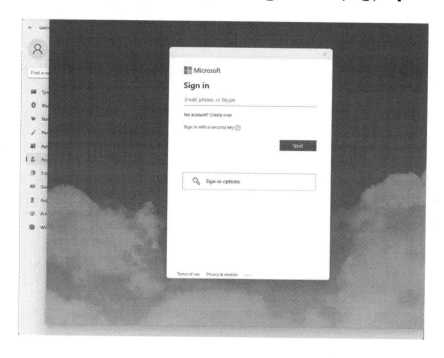

Figure 14

After that finishes up, your email account is synced to your device, and you are ready to receive and send emails and attachments.

Figure 15

The accounts tab is where your primary email account is listed, as well as any other email accounts that might be added to the device. From here, if you wish to send an email, all you will need to do is click on the new mail tab, and a window will pop up. There are going to be spaces for adding the recipient's email address, if you would like to copy the email and send it to someone else, you can add that person's email address in the CC line, which just means carbon copy. There is also a subject line where you can put what the email is regarding, and then there is just the space left for you to write your message.

If you would like to add pictures or files as an attachment to the email, usually there is a paper clip or just a plus sign depending on which email provider you use, and then you can add files from your computer. It will pop up a box and give you locations on your computer where the file might be stored. For example: if it's on your desktop, like a picture you grabbed from a website that you just dragged and dropped, or if it's in your documents folder because it's the recipe for your mother's Lemon Ice Box Pie and you want to share it with your granddaughter. Select the file you desire to send, and click add or attach. Again, the terminology may change a bit over the differ t services, but they all follow the same train of thought.

After you finish composing your message, all that's left to do is hit send, and your letter is going to make its way through the Internet within milliseconds and heading straight for your recipient.

Now, there are various folders to be aware of with any email account. Let's see briefly a little about what each of these is.

Inbox: this is where all of the incoming emails that are sent to you appear, messages from family/friends, order updates on online purchases, advertising emails, and newsletters from your favorite authors. You catch my drift here, pretty much anything that is addressed to you shows up here.

Outbox or Sent: here, you can find what emails you have sent to other people, it will give you the date, and the time it was sent. I tend to check this folder if someone says they didn't receive an email to double-check it did indeed send, and if it did, I could just copy and paste the information over so I don't have to type it out again.

Drafts: here is where things can be both a lifesaver and where if someone says they didn't get an email, and you don't see it in the Sent folder, and then it's probably still here in Drafts. This folder contains all the unsent emails that have some content. Either you started emailing someone and got called away, so you weren't able to finish composing the message, or that you lost internet connection and it just saved it for you to return to later. You can even click directly from the email you are working on and hit save to drafts, but the majority of all email providers auto-save your progress while writing your message, so it's more streamlined.

Spam: finally, here is the dreaded black hole that sucks your time away if you let it. All email providers have a spam filter that is supposed to filter out all of your emails that either look like a scam or emails from companies who have gotten ahold of your email address, marketing campaigns...etc. If this filter is triggered, your provider just drops the message into your spam folder. For the most part, it works like it needs to, but on rare occasions, it will drop an email that you might be waiting for into this folder instead of in your inbox. So, it's a nice idea to periodically check this folder to make sure you haven't missed anything vital. For most accounts, you won't have to go through and delete each message, they give you a bulk delete option, or in most cases, the provider goes ahead and deletes the contents of this folder every 30 days.

Gmail Accounts

Since we briefly touched upon this earlier I want to talk a little about using your Gmail account if you decide to set up your email account through them. If you set up a Google Account when you first downloaded Google Chrome, you likely already have a Gmail account set up. Now, whether you want to use it or not is another story, personally, I have used a Gmail account for all of my personal and business accounts for the last decade, and I really enjoy the user-friendly web version and as well now easy it is to use on a mobile device or my tablet. You get timely notifications when you have a new email. You can prioritize if there are certain email addresses you want to know immediately. You can do this either through extra sounds or notification banners being set to your computer or phone if you have your email set up on your phone.

I also like the ability to set my do not disturb settings to where I do not get notified of new messages within a specific time frame. Usually, I set this to when I know I will be asleep, so I don't hear my computer constantly pinging with new messages if I forget to shut it down when I leave my home office at night.

Email Scams

Unfortunately, we cannot have a chapter on emailing without talking about the potential scam or phishing emails you might receive. The majority of these are caught and put into your spam folder, but with some of the new sophisticated scams, they can land straight in your inbox, and they are nearly impossible to determine if it's a legitimate email or one designed to get your financial information or other information you don't want floating around out in cyberspace.

The new scams will pretend they are from your banking institution and say there are unauthorized users or charges on your account and that you must email them back and provide your account number, debit card number, PIN number...etc. Your bank will not typically email you regarding these situations, they will call you, and there is a process to go through. If you get an email like that one from your credit card company or bank, I always call to verify first before providing any information. The same thing can be said with the Social Security Administration. They do not just send you an email, and they will either call or send a letter by US Mail for any information requests or to let you know there is an issue that needs your attention.

It's common in these types of emails they are just looking for account information. They will use the same logos and branding to make you think it is a legitimate email, but there are always subtle differences, a company name is misspelled, or the email itself is littered with poor grammar and misused words. In addition, the email address states nothing like @amazon.com or the business or entity they are trying to impersonate. If you want, you can report these scams to the FTC.

Final Thoughts

While I still think that nothing can beat sending a physical letter, you can't deny the appeal of just logging on and sending a quick note, being able to be notified when your online order has shipped, and how to track where the package is. The email has really opened up a huge communication pathway that connects us worldwide. Some people say advances in technology have taken us farther apart as a human race, but I think in this aspect it has united us more than ever. Like we talked about with security while browsing the web, staying vigilant with your email communications is also a huge aspect of being safe while being connected to the world.

CHAPTER 6

Link and Use Other Devices

So you've got your computer all set up, you have your email and other accounts all up and running, and you have your apps downloaded so you can enjoy a nice game of Bunco later on. What more to life is there, right?

Well, your computer is just part of the puzzle. There are countless other devices that you can connect your device to that will give you even more options. Most devices now connect to your computer with a wireless connection called Bluetooth. If you remember we discussed this capability earlier in the book. You can find the settings by clicking on start and going to settings, or sometimes you can find the Bluetooth icon to the left of the time and date at the bottom of the screen.

That little blue circle with the odd little symbol on it is where you will find your Bluetooth settings. Most devices, from your phone to your TV to even your fitness tracker or insulin pump, have Bluetooth capability to them. This allows the devices to communicate wirelessly to share information. The days of having various wires and cords snaking out to your keyboard, mouse, printer, and modem are gone. Everything is a lot more streamlined, which makes it nice.

Figure 16

So, once you click on the Bluetooth icon, or if you like, you can look for the Start menu, then click on Settings, which gives you more options. Once you are there, a tab will appear saying Bluetooth & Devices (Figure 16). There is a graphic on the following page we will be working from to walk through the rest of the examples.

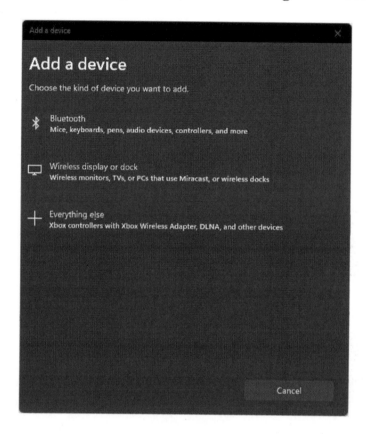

Figure 17

First of all, you should be sure that the Bluetooth connection is turned on. You'll want to check this on your computer. If there's a Bluetooth setting on, the device you are trying to pair with your computer, like with a mouse, or keyboard, you will find in the settings a Bluetooth on and off switch.

Figure 18

But for this specific example, we will stick with the basics. After ensuring your connection is turned on, where you see that devices tab, go ahead and click on that. In that area, you can begin to pair your new device or check settings on devices already paired with your computer if someone else sets them up for you, like a friend or family member.

If pairing a new device, just click on that add device, and the computer will scan for nearby devices that have an operating Bluetooth connection. Choose the kind of device you want to connect and then look for the name of the device you wish to pair with your computer, like a printer for example, and click on the icon listed as the graphic on the previous pages will show. There will be a few prompts, with some devices, it may even ask you to confirm the code that is displayed on both the device itself and your computer. But other items just connect once you click on the icon to confirm the pairing. After the connection has been established, your computer will let you know that the pairing was successful and that you are ready to use your new device with your computer.

Here's something important to note, how to connect/disconnect devices after you already have them paired with your computer. Remember that toggle switch where we turned on our Bluetooth capability earlier, well you can turn this on and off, you don't always have to keep it connected. Once you turn it back on, if the device you had previously connected is turned on and close by it will automatically connect to your computer.

But if for some reason, the paired device doesn't work the way it should, or you just want to turn it off, you can disconnect the device from the computer, just press on the three dots positioned on the right-hand side of the pane where the device is listed and hit disconnect. With that, the device's connection to your computer is severed until the next time you power it back on or reconnect it to your computer. In the graphic presented on the previous page, the only thing that changes if you want to connect a previously connected device is where it says disconnect; it will now say connect.

If you experience trouble after disconnecting and reconnecting the device doesn't fix the issue, you can also click on the remove device and then just pair it with your computer again. Sometimes this fixes the problem. I had a printer once that I had to use that trick on almost every time I used it, so I became well versed in that procedure.

Also, if you get a different device or no longer use a device listed in that portion of the Bluetooth settings you can just click remove device to keep things from becoming too cluttered.

And the mystery is solved, really that's all there is to it. Your devices should be all connected and ready to use. In today's day and age, almost every device in our homes has a Bluetooth connection with it. I have even seen a Crock-Pot that would connect to your Wi-Fi connection through Bluetooth, and you could turn the Crock-Pot on and off through an app through your phone while you were out of the house. And at that point, I honestly thought I had seen it all! But like I mentioned with the apps, if you can think it up, and it seems like there's a need for it, someone is probably working on it to make sure it requires tasks less work.

CHAPTER 7

Working With Photos & Videos

Remember when I said there is an app or software for anything you might want to do? Well, there are some great apps for photo projects. These are useful to organize snapshots you have in albums or photo boxes. Most of those apps cost money, and they can be a little intimidating to start using unless you have prior experience with such tasks. One of the major advancements in this new version of Windows is the Photos software that is already built in.

Figure 19

If you navigate to the start menu, you can find the Photos app pretty simply, I have it set on my pinned menu, just so you can see what the icon looks like, and for you to locate it on your own computer, all you have to do is type in the search bar, and away you go!

Once you click on that icon, you will have a lot of different options to choose from. You can edit your photos and then organize them into collections, or just allow Windows to organize them for you and place them in themed albums, like they will put all of your Christmas pictures together or all of your pet photos. They even offer you the capability to organize your photos by who is in them, so you can have all your photos with your grandson John all in one place. There are a lot of different options available. A lot of your navigation comes from a bar that looks like this:

Figure 20

going from left to right, this bar that appears when you have a picture selected will allow you to group/favorite your photo. This is provided by the first icon. You can zoom in and out with the next two. You can revert the photo with the following icon, while the icon with the pencil and the photo will allow you to edit your picture. Next, we have delete with the trash can, the heart will allow you to add the photo to your favorites which then store it in a specific album, and the icon with the "I" in a circle gives you all the important information about the photo. Then as you have learned from other sections, the three dots always means that there are a few more options here in case you haven't found what you are looking for.

Options in the drop-down give you more actions like:

- Printing the selected photo

- Resizing the photo

- Starting a slideshow of the images you currently have either in that particular album or on your device.

Editing a Photo

So to edit a photo, click to open the specific picture you would like to work on. A toolbar with three icons will appear at the top of the image. Starting from the left side, the first icon is where you can edit aspects of the photo, like cropping the picture, which is essentially selecting certain elements you would like to focus on and cutting out what you don't want to be seen in the final image. For example, I took a picture of my rose bush next to my deck, but my dog got in the picture. Now, if I only want to focus on the rose bush, I can take the cropping tool, and it will give you a box to click and drag to show only what you want to see.

Under the editing tab, you can also adjust the brightness of an image, and pretty much the coolest thing ever is to remove red eyes from a photo. For those who remember snapshots or days gone by, red eyes happen! And nothing ruins a picture quicker than looking like you are possessed.

The next icon allows you to write or add text to your pictures. These are great if you want to write a personal message, like for a birthday or anniversary.

And then, the third icon you have allows you to use a filter on your image. Filters are an easy way to edit your pictures. They are preset with certain setting levels like contrast, brightness, and sharpness; think of this as when you would have to adjust your television to get the best picture. You can even turn photos in color to black and white with the click of a mouse. Playing with filters is always a fun way to give new life to older photos that you may have seen a thousand times before, but you'd like to provide them with a more modern vibe.

If you see the two arrows next to the other icons, these are an undo and redo changes. So let's say you turned the picture of your granddaughter in her cap and gown into a black and white photograph, but once it's done, you would rather turn it back into the original. You can do this by hitting the arrow on the left: this will undo any recent changes to the image. The arrow on the right will redo a recently made change.

Once you get all of the changes made, all you have to do is go up to where the three dots are and click to view the drop-down menus. There will be an option that says Save a Copy, and you will be able to save a new copy of the file with the artistic changes you made to the image.

Making a New Folder

So, now that you have all these images on your computer, you probably want to group them, right? Like we talked about earlier, Windows will take some of the work off your shoulders and organize them how they see fit. But if you want to make an album of your own, let's say you took a trip to Florida to see the beach. You want to put all your pictures from that trip into one folder. So all you do, from the main screen where you see thumbnails of all your images, find the icon at the top right side of the software that looks like two images together. That will be a drop-down menu. Click on that; it will provide you with a list of actions. Click where it says album, and that will allow you to create and name a new album and select which pictures you want to group in that album.

All you have to do is to select an image is click on the check box at the corner of each image file you would like to include in the album. When you have all of them selected, there will be a button that says Create, so just click on that, and you will officially have created your first photo album.

Figure 21

Working from the main screen of the Photos software you will see a toolbar that looks like this (Figure 21). I wanted to take some time to point out how to access certain aspects of your photos.

Collection is the list of albums Windows groups together.

Albums are the ones you create, like the example we just walked through with your vacation pictures.

People is where if you have the switch in the on position Windows will go through and use facial recognition software to group all the pictures of your grandson currently on your computer in one folder. Note, this will even work if you took a screenshot or screen grab from a news article.

Folders are the various areas you have image files.

And then the **Video Editor** if you would like to put together a video project using either video files you have imported onto your device or just putting together a project using a combination of pictures and video files. These are great for making videos for a retirement party, or an anniversary.

You can also see the location of the double image icon that we previously discussed on the top right side after the search bar. Also, one more icon to look at is that icon right before the infamous three dots. With that icon you can import pictures. For example, if you have a digital camera, you can just select that icon and it will walk you through connecting your device. This works either through Bluetooth, or by a USB cable used to download pictures off of the camera to store them on your computer.

Finally, you can filter the images shown by clicking on the view by drop-down menu. It will allow you to see images taken on a certain date, by file type. Maybe you only want to see video files you have on your device; click there, and it will show only what you want to know if you want to be specific and not need to check all the thumbnails of pictures and videos to find what you are looking for.

Another easy way to search, as always, is by utilizing our handy friend, the search bar. Type in the album, person, or whichever unique information the image file may contain.

Final Thoughts

As you can see from our discussions in this chapter, some new features makes the Photos software that comes already preinstalled on your computer a thousand times better than any of the older Windows versions.

Windows 11 offers us a program comparable to some of those expensive photo editing apps that everyone always talks about, and in my opinion, this is a lot more intuitive and user-friendly.

With the Photos app, you can organize your photos, edit them for a more modern/artistic feel, and you can import and backup your original physical photos because it never hurts to have backups for those priceless memories and life events that take place in those beloved pictures.

CHAPTER 8

Tips and Tricks

So, how are we feeling about branching out into technology? Feeling pretty comfortable, I hope. I know you are doing great, and getting what you need to be done all lined out. What level of Candy Crush are you on already? We are about to kick off our final chapter of the book by talking about some tips and tricks that will take all of the knowledge you have gleaned from this book and kick it up a notch.

There are the final little tidbits it might be important to know or just fun to brag about that you figured out. People give seniors a lot of flack for stereotypically being less tech-friendly, which I don't get at all. If you started this book and you had a computer sitting in front of you but haven't done anything more than taking it out of the box, you made that first step, you decided to go out and educate yourself instead of just saying it was going to be too hard, or that it wasn't your cup of tea.

My goal for this project was to show people of all skill levels that there are things you can still learn, especially with a newer version of Windows, because with each version that has come out within the last 36 years or so, there are always new features and advances, new programs to try. Your education in Windows is a constantly evolving thing. That's like saying I was a master at Windows 3.1 because that's the first system I used. Let me tell you...a lot changed since back then, and I'm still learning new things every day about Windows 11 and how I can customize it to my day-to-day life. As my life changes and as I get older, my tech needs change too, so my today's settings, might not be my settings tomorrow.

So, let's jump right into talking about these last final pieces of the puzzle to get you on your way to become a tech-savvy senior.

<u>Moving Start & Taskbar</u>: this one is a huge customization for your computer. This is the first Windows version where these components have moved from their traditional spots. And some people like it, but if you would like to change it, it's easy to switch around in four simple steps.

- Right-click on the bar and select **Taskbar Settings**.

- Or you can also go to **Settings** > **Personalization** > **Taskbar** to access the settings necessary to make these changes.

- Look down the page and find the area that says **Taskbar behaviors**.

- Select the menu that mentions taskbar alignment and select **Left**. Your Taskbar will now slide over to the left.

<u>Opening the Task Manager</u>: If you have used any version of Windows prior, you know that sometimes you need the Task Manager in order to force a program that is not functioning to close so you can restart it to get it working again. All technology experiences glitches, so it's important to know how to get to this resource. The Task Manager window will show you everything that is currently processing on your computer.

To find this, all you have to do is right-click on the Start menu, and there will be some options that pop up. Click on **Task Manager**, and then a window will pop up. Just find the program's name that has stopped responding and select it, and there should be a force close or force stop option to end the process. This is an invaluable tool if you want to learn to troubleshoot and fix simple issues instead of waiting on a friend or family member to resolve the issue or spending hours on hold with a tech support line. It's your front line of figuring things out, it's not going to be the cure-all for every issue, but it's a good place to start. You can also activate the Task Manager by pressing and holding together three keyboard commands: CTRL + ALT + DEL

<u>Add Often Used Folders to The Start Menu</u>: On previous versions of Windows you could put the folders that you use a lot, like Documents or Photos right there on your start menu. You didn't have to go through a few steps to get them there. With Windows 11, you now have to go through a bit of a process, but thankfully it's pretty simple.

- Press Win + I to open the **Settings tab**.

- Click on **Personalization**.

- Next, click on where it says **Start** and then on **Folders**.

Once you make it to this tab, you can customize which folders will show up on Start located next to the Power icon. To add a folder, just move the switch for each folder and set it to On or Off depending on your preference.

<u>Change Your Quick Settings</u>: remember when we talked about accessing the quick settings on the taskbar by the time and date, you can change what setting and information is displayed there. This is another customization option that helps you fine-tune your computer only to show the information and settings you are interested in. To change what is displayed, all you have to do to modify these panes are:

- Click on the Time and Date zone to bring up the Notification panel as well as the Calendar.

- Click on the icon displaying **Network, Speaker, and Battery** to see where all the settings are listed. Here you'll find your screen brightness and volume controls, connectivity options (Wi-Fi and Bluetooth), and other accessibility features.

- Lastly, if you want to shift anything in and out just click the Pencil to add other components. Next, click on Add and select the option you would like to add to this section. You should now click on the pin to remove it from the pane if it's already listed.

App Hopping: If you are anything like me, I usually have a few different apps open at one time while I'm at my computer. And stopping and clicking on the icon to bring each one up again can be a pain in the posterior. A simple way to see what apps you have running and switch back and forth between them is just a couple of keystrokes away.

- To see what apps are running, press the CTRL + TAB key at the same time, so you are able to see all the open apps.

- To shift between your open apps, use one of the Arrow or Tab keys. If you prefer, you can use the CTRL + TAB keyboard shortcut to switch quickly to different apps in the order you most recently used them.

Utilizing Dark Mode: as I'm sure you noticed, I use dark mode a lot on my personal and work computers. I find it's a little easier on my eyes than staring at all of the glaring white space all day. But I find it easier on my eyes to have it darker. Here's how to activate Dark Mode and the cool new feature of Windows 11, the Night Light feature.

- **Dark Mode**: go to **Settings** > **System** > **Personalization** > **Colors**. Then, click the drop-down menu and where it says **Choose your mode** and select **Dark**.

- **Night-Light**: if you happen to find yourself working long hours, you can use the Night Light setting. When this one is turned on, it basically filters out the harmful blue light by transforming it into warmer colors. All you need to do to make it turn on is navigate to **Settings** > **System** > **Display**.

Pin Apps to The Start Menu: to easily access your favorite apps, because they probably won't all fit on your taskbar, and it's less cluttered that way, you can just pin our most-used apps to appear when you click on Start. All you have to do to pin an app is open the App list, then right-click on the app you want to add to the Start menus and click Add to Start. Then it will be right there and easy to find.

<u>Checking Battery Usage</u>: some apps tend to use more battery power than others. You might want to make sure they are closed if you are planning on having to conserve your available battery. But how do you find out what processes are using what? Go to **Settings** > **System** > **Power & battery**, then click on the **Battery Usage tab**. In this area, there will be a chart that displays how much power you have used over a specific amount of time. Towards the bottom of this window, there will be all of your apps and it shows how much battery is utilized by that individual app. If you find something that is draining too much power, it gives you the capability to close down the background usage and lessen some of the demand on the battery.

<u>Make Text Bigger</u>: I know I use this setting pretty often if I forget my glasses, or I just don't want to put them on. It will make all of the text on your screen larger and easier to see. All you have to do is click on the Start Menu, and click on **Settings**. Once there, you'll see an accessibility tab. Click on where it says text size and adjust it to your preferences.

<u>Take A Screenshot</u>: this is an important action, one that I find pretty handy, I screenshot order receipts and chat messages, even if I want to remember my place on the book I was reading on my laptop. There are a lot of different usages. If you want to take a picture of your entire screen, all you have to do is on your keyboard and hit the Print Screen key along with the Windows key at the same time. Your computer will automatically save this picture in your Pictures folder and in the Screenshots tab.

If you only want to take a picture of a certain area of your screen then you just have to push the Windows icon on your keyboard + Shift + S to open a program named **Snip & Sketch**. This software will allow you to click and drag to produce a screenshot of just the specific area, and then it will save it to the clipboard.

Check Your Storage: remember earlier when I mentioned that having too many apps might make your computer run slower than necessary. Well, I bet you were wondering how we figure out how much space is currently occupied. Here's how to find out: **Settings** > **System** > **Storage**. Click on the button that mentions showing more categories to show you a list of what is taking up your precious space. If you happen to be running low, there is a button that says **Cleanup Recommendations**, and that's Windows performing an analysis of what programs are using what and how often you use them. If you see something like a game you haven't played in a while, it's safe to say you could take that off of there to help speed things up.

Battery Saver: this goes hand in hand with our other tip on figuring out if you have programs consuming more battery than others. On every device, there are processes always running. Even though you are not using the program or app at that moment, it's still drawing power and functioning in the background. So, to control which apps are running and save your battery, go to **Settings** > **System** > **Power & Battery**. Click where it says **Battery Saver**, and then you can determine when the battery saver kicks on to limit some notifications and background activity when you may not be near a charger to plug in.

Final Thoughts

And now we have reached the end of all of the top tips and tricks to impress all your friends and family members. There are some other great resources online with more customization options, and keystroke commands to make navigating through your computer easier. However, for the very introductory aspect of this book, I wanted to keep things simple. Sometimes the keystroke commands may seem like a game of Twister for your hands and I know those with limited mobility may find them frustrating. I'll just leave it as if you would like to learn more, doing a quick search on Google or your most favorite search engine for key shortcuts for Windows 11 will bring up more options for you to continue your journey with learning all of the ins and outs regarding Windows.

There are further customizations like changing the theme of your computer and changing the default settings that you can find just by exploring some of the areas we have already visited. You just have to take a look around and see what you might like to change to fine-tune your computer into running the way you would like and looking the way you want.

Conclusion

We made it to the end! We covered a lot of ground since we started together on the first page, and I hope we could ease some of the hesitations you might have experienced when you were sitting there faced with your computer, and going: "so, what do I do now?"

During the course of this book, you have learned the basic fundamentals of operating your computer, how to customize the settings, which apps are helpful in your day-to-day life, creating your own e-mail accounts and downloading essential software. Even some basic troubleshooting tactics in case something starts to malfunction.

You should be exceedingly proud of the progress you have made. Learning about technology is not an easy subject. It's one of the few industries where they have their own language. But by taking all of the jargon out of it, or as much as we can, it makes the process easier and it makes very simple the process of learning and retaining the information.

Microsoft is continually making changes and making new strides in the existing Windows 11 and making plans for their next version, whatever it may be titled. One thing we certainly know is that they will continue to have their collective fingers on the pulse of the new features that the world craves and is looking for. The bar has been set pretty high as far as I'm concerned with this operating system, but as history has shown, the only place you can go from here is up! Just remember the interface for Windows 1.

Made in the USA
Middletown, DE
19 April 2023

29113885R00042